PAWS

and

People

By: David Laubert, DVM

DEDICATION

I want to thank the countless pets and owners I have met over the years. They have literally provided the substance for this book. Any names used in these stories are not the actual names of pets nor owners. Thank you also to the many family and friends who have encouraged me to pursue putting all these true stories together in a way to share them. I hope the readers gain insight into the quirky field of veterinary medicine, but also hope that you can laugh, maybe cry, and truly appreciate your veterinarian on a whole new level.

Part One

There is, sometimes, humor during an euthanasia...

In response to the elderly husband's question: Me: Yes, it actually is very peaceful.

Elderly Wife: Remember, honey, when my heart stopped, and I fell and hit my head on the toilet? It didn't hurt, and I didn't feel a thing.

Client: When my dog lays down, her stomach makes these little bubble noises.

Me: Like a gurgling noise?

Client: No, like a bubble popping kind of noise.

Me: Are you sure she's not just farting when she lays down?

<Seemed like a logical question to me!>

Flashback humor from yesterday:

Vet Tech, in disbelief: The cat in this room had kittens in July, and the kittens are STILL nursing.

Me: Go back in there and bite that woman's nipple and tell her that is what her cat is feeling when the kittens are nursing.

True story...dog goes to groomer for a shampoo, comes to us after having jumped out of the kennel, and very likely ruptures its cranial cruciate ligament--and the owner finds out from ME, not the groomer, that it happened when the dog jumped out of the kennel. The owner was simply asked when told the pet was

done with her shampoo, "Was your pet limping this morning, because she is limping now?" Really?! Really?!

Funny moment of the week:

In a room by myself with clients who only speak Spanish, they are here to get booster vaccines for their cute little puppy. I open the door to ask one of the receptionists to hold for me while I give the vaccines, but I realize I have grabbed the wrong one. So I leave the room and come back to find the receptionist talking about the pets his family had when he was younger, the breeds of the dogs, etc. IN ENGLISH. And I am amused at the politeness of the clients who are simply smiling and nodding at him.

Okay, so I might have accidentally said out loud what I was thinking in my head when a client said, "I know, maybe I am just really paranoid about my pet", and I responded, "So what you are saying is YOU are the one who really needs a doctor, not your pet?" Oops, but thankfully, she laughed and agreed

Me: There are adult fleas on your dog.

Client: I know, our other dog is even more itchy than this one.

~~later in the conversation~~

Me: You are going to have to treat your house because once you treat your dogs, the fleas are going to be coming after you for a blood meal. For example, you might notice little bites on your ankles, like red spots.

Client: Oh, we already have those.

Me (almost out loud): TREAT YOUR DAMN HOUSE ALREADY! REALLY?

Awkward moment in exam room with an older woman when pet decided to clean itself: Client to pet: "Why are you licking your TW*#. Huh? Quit licking your TW*#!

Me: Speechless, really.

Fun from the week:

Client via phone: So, is my cat supposed to be licking his area a lot after his neuter?

Employee: Has he been wearing the e-collar?
Client: No, I took it off after the first day

Subsequent cost to client: antibiotics, additional pain meds, and one angry, painful kitten!

Realizing a pet has chewed her IV catheter out, leaving a big portion of it still IN the vein=sharting in your scrubs.

Having your co-worker do her first cut-down and retrieving it=priceless

Murphy's law of "first day back at work from vacation": Hit by a car arriving about 40 minutes before closing time

My day at work would be sooooo awful without the wonderful vet techs and front desk staff!!

An owner calls to say her dog is bleeding from the mouth. They come right in (because they called from the parking lot), and there is no blood in the mouth, but blood around the rectum. The diagnostic test shows Clostridium-like organisms (abnormal bacteria) and a small amount of blood in the poop.

Client: Ok, well, I will be honest. I gave him lamb and cabbage yesterday because I was cooking it, and he really wanted some. First time I ever gave it to him. I am having a dinner party today and didn't want to have to deal with this and my guests, too. Can you stop it?

Bubble of my head: Lady, I am pretty sure lamb and cabbage would give ME bloody poop. Just saying... and let me get my wand from the treatment room, and I will stop it right now.

Client: I didn't want another dog after my previous dog died, but my son gave me this one. How long can this kind of dog (a 4-year-old Shih Tzu) live? Like maybe 10 years?

Me: Well, it varies a lot, of course, but we do have some small breed dogs like yours that come here who are 12-15 years old or so.

Client: Oh! That is too long for a dog to live.

My thought bubble: Uh, wait, what?

Client: "Both my cat and I had thyroid cancer. They cut me here and here (pointing to the

scars on either side of the neck) and opened me up like a Pez dispenser."

Client: So, don't you have a discount or payment plan for poor, crippled people like me?

Me, but only in my head: Okay, can't believe you really just used the word "crippled" when you walked in here and have full function of both arms and legs, and no, we don't even have those for rich, healthy people.

More over-sharing in the exam room:

Client: My dog has terrible gas. I think he learned that from me. After my gastric by-pass surgery, I farted so bad it scared my dog, and I live alone, so if I had to fart, I just farted--now he farts."

Best client encounter of the day, from an Irishman (with dogs named Stout and Guiness), speaking with a great Irish accent...expressing his frustration over figuring out what was causing his dog's hot spots--"It's like putting an Irishman in a round room and telling him the free beer is in the corner."

Client encounter today...

Me: "So what concerns do you have today with Charlie?"

Client: "Well, I just can't keep him from watching the porn channel on TV."

Bubble over my head: "Wtf?"

Best client education from the past week:

Although I can sort of understand the thought process, if you think your dog has a yeast infection in his ear, your best bet for treatment is NOT to instill a human feminine hygiene product in your dog's ear. Just saying...

Another episode of "Yep, that really happened":

Vet tech: The doctor will want to do at least a skin impression <and other diagnostics> once he clips the matted hair off the lesion and can see the whole extent of the lesion.

Client: Can't he just smell it and tell me if there is an infection going on?

Me to the Tech: Do you double-dog dare me? Because I may or may not have actually cracked an egg over my 4th-grade teacher's head because of a dare.

Exam room conversation yesterday with mother and daughter:

Mother: My daughter (who clearly looks a little pale) needs to run to Taco Bell, she graduated high school yesterday, and she was at a party last night--she's hungover.

Me (to the daughter): Oh, congratulations on graduating

Client: Man, so many parties this week, I think I have been drunk 4 nights this week.

Me: <no response needed>

Okay, so if I have to use drugs to very possibly save your dog's life from a potentially life-threatening arrhythmia while it's under anesthesia, calling to yell at me and my staff AND dropping the f-bomb multiple times because I have the nerve to charge you (approx. $40) for those drugs, makes me think

A) You are an idiot, and is your dog's life really not worth $40 to keep him in your life? Mean people suck!

So if your logic behind not wanting core vaccines for your pet is "I have a friend who is a veterinarian, and he says most people over-vaccinate their pets", then my question to you is, "Why aren't you taking your pet to your friend who is a veterinarian instead of coming to see me?" Just saying...

Man approaches the front desk just after closing:

He, in a heavy accent: Excuse me, doctor, can I ask you a question? (damn, left my white coat on)

Me: Sure (not always a good response, just saying...)

Him: Can you recommend a flea and tick medicine for my <some blend of coat/dog/cat>?

Me: I'm sorry, did you say for your dog (good guess anyway)?

Him: No, for my goat.

Me: truly speechless for like the 3rd time ever in my life.

I talked to a group of elementary school kids yesterday about being a veterinarian...

Student: How long did you have to go to school?

Me: About 8 years (followed by oohs and ahhs from the students)

Student: Wow, that's a long time.

Different Student: Geez, if you started school when I was born, you would just be finishing school now.

Client misconnect of the week: So after explaining to a client the possibility that his dog might have an endocrine disease called hyperadrenocorticism, and referring to it as Cushing's Disease, explaining what the disease is, and recommending testing for it and why..."Well, I don't think we need to test for that. He has always been very active and hyper his whole life."

Best client comment of the week..."I need to know if my dog is a chihuahua or a canine." Hm...

There's always something so strangely ironic with the juxtaposition of a first visit/puppy room followed by an old dog euthanasia room...the circle of life all within 30 minutes.

Great room yesterday when the breeder accompanied the new owner on the first visit with the puppy:

Breeder: I usually recommend giving only half the vaccine dose to puppies because they don't need the same amount as an adult dog.

Bubble over my head: Do you have any idea how the immune system works?

Breeder: Well, if you don't breed them (the males), they won't start to mark their territory, so you don't really have to neuter them.

Bubble over my head: And who told you that? Betty Crocker?

Ah, the glamorous side of veterinary medicine...literally kneeled unknowingly (at first) in a pile of dog poop, and had to bathe a dog (before his neuter) that had pooped in his kennel and then decided to "finger paint" the kennel. Good times!

At approximately 6 pm today, with a dog that is presenting with serious increased/abdominal effort breathing:

Client: "We are not really sure if my wife ran over her with the car, or hit her, but it happened about 2-3 hours ago. We got concerned when my wife gave the dog some aspirin in some cheese a little while ago, and she threw it up with some blood. And the way she's breathing...it's really not normal for her."

Seriously! You waited until she threw up blood to be concerned that your wife somehow hit your pet with the car?! Well, welcome to a pneumothorax...now your dog needs to have the air evacuated from its thorax so its lungs can actually inflate properly. If it were your child, would you have waited until your child vomited blood to be concerned? Geez people!!!!!

After declining hospitalization and full treatment for her unvaccinated, parvo-positive puppy because of financial constraints:

Client: "We want to get her vaccinated when she's better, but not spayed because we want her to have a life."

Me (hoping my face hides my true thoughts): "A life? What do you mean?"

Client: "We want her to be a mom and have puppies so we can have one of her puppies when she is gone."

Me: "Please visit a shelter before you consider NOT spaying her. There are tons of homeless puppies; many are there because owners didn't realize how expensive it would be to fully care for and vaccinate them until they find homes, assuming they all find homes. And there is always the risk of pyometra (inserting full explanation here) in an unspayed female, which almost always results in emergency surgery."

Client: "You are kind of scaring me."

Me in my head: "Good, because if you had vaccinated her in the first place, this current situation never would have happened, plus your puppy may not live long enough even to have puppies."

Real me: "I am sorry if I'm scaring you, and that's not my intent, but I just want you to be aware of what could happen."

After explaining again the health and behavior benefits of neutering their already aggressive little dog, one teenage son asks, "What does neutering actually mean?", while one teenage daughter then asks, "Well, won't he be sad?" Which prompts me to ask, "Why do you think he would be sad?" Her reply, "Because he will know they are not there anymore."

Client: "I brought my dog in because I think he has ringworm by his nose, but I have never actually seen ringworm before, and I don't know what it looks like."

After offering to do a fungal culture to verify, and telling said client that it honestly looks like a scab from an old abrasion that is about to fall off ...

Client: "So if it is ringworm, can I just buy some jock itch medicine and put it on there?"

Best client comment of the past week (this stuff really can't be scripted any better!):

"I don't think my other dog is fat or overweight, really. I just think his body is bigger than his head, like his head is too small or something."

Client's 20-year-old daughter: Are you sure my dog is a female, because she is doing some male things like humping...

Me: (quickly glancing at the record, at the patient's age and the patient's anatomy, and that the patient has been coming here for 3 months)... Yes, very certain your pet is a female...

Client's mother: (a short time later) So, how can you tell a male dog from a female dog?

Me: (bubble over head: wtf? Did you really just ask that?)

Uh, just saying that the absence of a penis and testicles really sincerely confirms that your pet is NOT a male.

So yesterday, a geriatric dog presented with black diarrhea. The owner said, "At first I was worried because I thought it was black vomit, but I was relieved when I realized it was just black diarrhea." Really? Relieved? As it turns out (and this will mean more to vet med friends), BUN=128 and creatinine=7.2.

Client: So, when will my dog go into heat? He's already humping everything.

Bubble over my head: Did she really just ask when her MALE intact puppy is going to go into heat?

Tactful response? Not so much--forgot to turn on the tact filter...

Client: Do you think my dog is overweight?

Me: If you look at him from above, you should see the outline of his chest, then a nice curve in to see a slimmer abdomen (insert nice "hourglass" sort of hand demonstration). Your dog's outline is more like, well...a tube."

--Thankfully followed by client laughing hysterically, and thanking me for my blunt honesty--

Client: I am trying to crate train my puppy.

Me: How is that going?

Client: Well, I don't like to keep her in there for very long because I know exactly what it's like to live in a cage...seriously, and it's not fun.

--awkward moment of silence—

In my head: I hope he means jail or prison and not an actual cage.

Client with intact male dog: So, do you have any suggestions for me to keep my dog from trying to hump my female dog? She just had a litter of puppies, and he won't leave her alone.

What I wanted to say: Uh, freakin' neuter him and spay her! ARGGGG!

Me: How is Matilda doing? Do you have any concerns?

Client: I don't know if this is normal, but my dog licks her poop as she is going to the bathroom.

Me: Do you mean she licks it or tries to eat it after she goes to the bathroom?

Client: No, she licks it as she is pooping.

Bubble over my head: Wow, what crazy flexibility

Best client questions all day..."Is there anything I can spray on my cat so that I won't be allergic to him?"

Client, discussing his pet's name: Her original name was Duke. I got him from a friend who told me Duke was a boy. I don't know if they thought her nipples felt like balls or what, but my first vet was like 'Duke" is really a Duchess.

What I wanted to ask: What the hell were they palpating that they thought the nipples were balls? Eek!

Uncomfortable-how am I supposed to respond to this moment of the day or possibly the year:

Older (than me) female Client: You have such a kind face, doc.

Me: Well, thank you very much.

Client: No, you really do. If you ever need a place to live, please come stay with me for at least a week so that I can get some sleep.

Wait, what!!? What the hell does that even mean?

Routine rectal today, feces felt a little funny, and I extracted 3-4 cigarette filters from the dog...

Me: So I found cigarette filters in your dog's feces. <explained due to the nicotine, these can be toxic to dogs, especially a small one like his>

Client: I know where he is getting them. My wife has been trying to quit smoking, but I now know she is smoking out behind the house and throwing the butts in the yard.

Also in today's news...a dog presenting for inappetence after a vaccine several days ago."

Client: I just wanted to bring him in to see if he is okay. He didn't feel well after his vaccine a few days ago, and, well, after you told him he was overweight and needed to lose weight, he didn't want to eat for a few days. But he actually lost 1 lb!

3:30 pm in the afternoon today...

While discharging a post-dental prophy patient, the vet tech gives very explicit discharge instructions, then the client says:

"Can you repeat all of that...(then in a much quieter voice) I have been drinking."

Client: She is protective of food and toys. We were at my son's house for Thanksgiving, and my grandson tried to grab a toy that was near my dog, and my dog tried to bite him; he really went after him.

Me with the tech: Often, it's as much about training kids how to behave with a dog as it is to train the dog. How old is your grandson?

Client: He's 22 years old.

Just when you think your face is NOT betraying your thoughts...a client with a dog with a recurrent honking cough:

Client: I am worried about the cough again. I went to a psychic, and she told me to watch my dog; she sees some sort of illness in the body

(while motioning in the chest area).

Me: <Silent> but apparently not so silent

Client: Don't look at me like that, my family gives me that same look.

Oops, I need to work on my poker face, I guess!

Older female client with a Shih Tzu puppy:

"I bought him a Furby stuffed animal, but all he wants to do is hump it. So now when I want him to get his Furby, I say, 'Go get your humpy dog!'"

A good example of why client education is important. Please make your pet's doctor accountable for providing you with the "why" behind the treatments...

Me: So I see your pet is on monthly heartworm tablets, that is great.

Client: Yes, she is, but how do they even get heartworms? No one ever told me; they just said my pet needed the medicine every month.

True story, I swear...

Client on phone: "Hi, I need to get the number of my dog's rabies tag because I got arrested and they confiscated my dog. I can't get it back without the tag number."

The tech who answered the phone: "Okay, what is your dog's name?"

Client (and I really am not kidding): "His name is 'Felony', but we haven't been there in a while."

Spent the day filling in at a different clinic, or as I like to call it...At the corner of "running your ass off with no lunch" and "wtf went on here before now?"

The juxtaposition of tragedy and humor in veterinary medicine never ceases to amaze me...the euthanasia in one room with a little girl (like 6 yrs old) and her older brothers (who were all there when I was explaining what was going to happen, but not present for the actual euthanasia) saying, "No more pain, right?", then going into another room where the owner tells you about her dog's "humpy dog" Furby.

Client overshare of the week:

Client (after drooling dog slobbers all over my arm): I am so sorry about that.

Me: Believe me, if that's the worst thing that lands on me today, that is a good day!

Client: I work in law enforcement in the prison system, so I know what you mean. One time, my partner and I were restraining this one guy who was taking off all his clothes, and my partner said, "Hey, that guy's testicles are lying on your leg.

Me: Oh, I guess you win then.

Moment of the day...

Client, totally over-possessive, crazy cat owner (sorry, cat lovers): So, are most clients like this with their pets (as she is cooing and snuggling her cat while we do the physical exam)?

Me: Many actually are...

Me to tech in the room as client's head is down on the exam table: <Head nodding NO, and worried look on my face>

So, we had a cat in today for a dental cleaning, his name was (honestly!) Jesus Christ Superstar. To promote dental health month, I suggested that we take a picture of him and his name, place it in the lobby with a sign that reads, "Even Jesus needs his teeth cleaned once a year."

Funny how every day things at work can end up being unexpectedly...unexpected:

Vet tech is clipping a dog's butt area so that the owner can keep it cleaner (dog has diarrhea). Innocent 2nd vet tech walks by, the dog shoots diarrhea onto the tech clipping, innocent tech vomits and subsequently pees her pants!

Client conversation after a dog with bloody diarrhea presents for having eaten rotisserie chicken:

Client, with a slight tone: Well, how could he get sick from eating chicken?

Me, with no tone (honestly): Depending on how long the food was sitting out, there can be various amounts of bacteria in the food.

Client, with tone and attitude: The chicken was in the refrigerator the whole time.

Me, at least what I wanted to say: Well, the chicken was OUT of said refrigerator at some point, unless your dog regularly helps himself to what's inside the refrigerator!

Seriously!!

I understand that we all imitate our pets sometimes, but at other times the imitations make it nearly impossible for me not to laugh out loud...

Client: Well, he isn't peeing or pooping. He goes outside and squats like he's going to poop, and then he's like [client imitating pet's face], but nothing happens.

One last rather emotional post from the week and then I promise I will post cheerier things...

Owners of a 2-year-old dog decided to euthanize their sweet little pet after it was diagnosed with a PPDH (Peritoneal-pericardial diaphragmatic hernia, no trauma involved, so likely congenital). The husband did not want to stay in the room for the euthanasia, so it was his wife and I. After the dog was euthanized, the wife told me, "One of our children died right after birth, and now she will be there to meet Roxie at the Rainbow Bridge."...call me officially emotionally drained for the week!

Difficult moment of the week:

While euthanizing a service dog, immediately before I administered the euthanasia solution, the owner and family collectively said to their dedicated animal, who literally gave his body to serve his owner, "You can go off-duty now."

Humorous moment of the week:

Me: Having your pet spayed will eliminate her heat cycle.

Client: You mean she's gonna have a period? I don't want that mess all over my house!

While discharging a neuter patient... Male owner: Man, I feel so bad for him.

Me: Well, they were his testicles, not yours, and he will be fine...so will you.

Male owner: Yeah, you're probably right. Anyway, I lost mine years ago when I got married. <awkward laugh>

Me: I hope you are figuratively speaking

"Confusion" in the exam room:

Me: We are going to clip the hair around the abscess, so if it drains more, the hair won't get matted again.

Client: I have no idea what you mean.

Me: We are going to clip the hair around the abscess, so if it drains more, the hair won't get matted again.

Client: Oh, okay.

Nothing like a parent's ability to multitask, even in the exam room with three stair-step-age little boys...

Me: So tell me what's been going on with <pet's name>

Mom in the room: He has just not been acting right.

Child: Quit spitting on me! Other child: I didn't do it!

Mom: Sit on the bench and behave...He hasn't been eating, not really drinking very much...I said sit on the bench!... and hasn't had much energy the last 2 days or so.

Keeping it real in the exam room:

Client: I told the tech that you are probably going to come in here and tell me my dog is too fat.

Me: Well, your dog is too fat. <Thankfully client laughed>

Client: Look, when she lays on her side, her leg doesn't lie flat on the floor.

Me: Well, your dog is too fat.

Client: Why does she need her anal glands expressed so often?

Me: I hate to keep going back to this, but your dog is too fat...

Misguided anger in the exam room...
(paraphrasing a bit here)

Client: I am very upset. Every vet I called (why were you calling other vets?) said my pet should have been treated with a sulfa drug, not the metronidazole the vet gave me. He has coccidia, and he should have been treated with something else.

Tech: Your pet didn't have coccidia; your pet had clostridium.

Client: Well, what's the difference?

Tech: Well, Clostridium is a bacterium, and the coccidia are an intestinal parasite.

Client: Oh, all I could remember is that it began with a "cah" sound.

Seriously!!

Another "oops, that was supposed to remain in the bubble over my head, but it didn't" moment:

Groomer brings a dog that has been accidentally cut while being groomed, the pet is bleeding only slightly, but clearly needs attending to...

Groomer: Do you think we can finish the grooming first before you do anything for him?

Me: Why? Do you think he'll be cut again, and I can just fix all the cuts at one time? No, you can't finish the grooming first.

Most adorable moment of the week so far: A small class of about 10 little 8yr-10yr old kids came by the clinic for a short tour...

Teacher: Does anyone have any questions for the doctor?

Little boy: Yes, I have a question. One of my fish drowned once. I found him floating on his back in the tank.

A conversation that brought to mind a famous scene in one of the original "Pink Panther" movies, where Peter Sellers asks, "Does your dog bite?"...

In the exam room with a dog marked as a biter/scratcher, but seemingly friendly and calm:

Me: Has your dog tried to bite someone on a previous visit?

Client: No, he hasn't bitten anyone...well, not since last time.

Humor in the face of tragedy--I had the unfortunate task yesterday of simultaneously euthanizing two pets (cats) from the same household. One at end-stage kidney disease, and the other in declining health from suspected liver/abdominal neoplasm.

After both cats had passed, everyone in the room was crying, and the owner looked around the room at everyone and then said, "Well, aren't we a happy bunch!" A much-needed quiet laugh from everyone ensued.

Stating the obvious in the exam room:

Client: Okay, so I know we shouldn't be feeding him any table food, but maybe if I hear it from you, it will make the difference.

Me: You shouldn't be giving your dog any table food.

Client: Well, okay then.

<Me in my head: Okay, maybe you just needed to hear that from someone in a whitecoat--whatever it takes!>

Humor from yesterday, another "the words left my mouth before I could stop them" moment or could also fall under the "client overshares" moment...a pet presenting after the owner saw blood when the pet was defecating:

Me: Let me take a look...(Vet tech is holding the pet that is standing on all four legs. Of course, I am lifting the pet's tail and am examining and lightly palpating the perianal area.)

Male owner: They do that to me when they do my prostate exam.

Me: Oh, they restrain you like this when they do your exam?

Thankfully, everyone laughed.

A good reason to carry a spare set up scrubs...routine dental, pet gets bradycardic, then decides to block, gets a little atropine and is fine, then blocks again-->more atropine and fine again; then, in a cruel twist of coincidence, one of the ECG leads falls off without me noticing at first, so the ECG flat lines...pretty sure I might have sharted. But alas, lead was put back on, and all was well in the cardiac world. Shew!

Misinformed client...

Me: I understand you feed him a raw diet.

Client: Yes, beef and chicken, ever since he was 6 months old, but he gets dry food, too.

Me: So, is it chicken breast that you feed him?

Client: Every part, really. But don't worry, it's raw because I know if I cook the chicken, the bones can splinter.

<Argh! Angry fist--the bones can splinter regardless!>

Confusion at check-in:

Receptionist: What's your pet's name?

Client: "King"

Receptionist: What's your last name?

Client: Wait, my last name or my dog's last name?

A "wish I could hit the unsend button"

moment--clients presenting their dog that

likely has an eye infection:

Me, upon entering the room: Hi, how are you

guys today?

Clients: Fine, but we're not your patient

today.

<laughter>

Me: <laughter> True, I can see you guys are

fine.

Client: Well, actually, I do have a prosthetic

eye.

<Me in my head: Of course you do, wtf!>

Speaking to a client about his concerns with his two dogs, one male and one female...another case of "Really?!!" or maybe "Let's ask the obvious question"...:

Client: My boy dog always tries to hump her.

Me: Is he neutered?

Client: <look of confusion> Well, I don't know. He's 3 years old.

Me: Well, does he still have testicles or not?

<Really!!>

Poor, confused, misinformed client, talking about his female pug:

Client: I think she's a lesbian.

Me: What would make you say that?

Client: Well, she lifts her leg when she pees.

Me, bubble over my head, but so close to verbalizing it: Okay, first, have you ever known a lesbian, and second, I think you meant she thinks she's a male dog, because I don't know any lesbian or any gay man, for that matter, that lifts his leg when he pees.

Ugh, just had to tell a client (whose dog died while being taken care of while she was on vacation) that the necropsy results indicate her pet died from complications from malnutrition/starvation, and now legally has to be investigated as a neglect case.

Keeping it real in the exam room, while talking to the owner about her severely matted dog and pointing out the skin infections developing under the mats:

Me: Your dog needs to be groomed as soon as possible.

Owner: Oh, well, I groom him at home.

Me: Ok, well, you are fired, and you need to take him to a professional groomer.

Exam room...pet presenting for a ~6cm ruptured mass at the base of the tail, I am palpating the mass and blood is dripping out (I surprisingly actually did put gloves on) ...

Vet tech, restraining the pet, and can't see fully:

Is it cheesy?

Female owner: That's gross. <husband laughs out loud>

Vet tech: We kind of live for this stuff.

Me: Yeah, we really do <me nodding in agreement, husband continues to laugh>

Pet: <on cue...shakes his hind end and a big blood clot comes flying out of the mass and lands on the floor> PRICELESS!

So not judging (harshly), but...client (mid-20s ish) with 7 yr old unspayed female and a 4.5 yr old un-neutered male:

Me: When was your female's last heat cycle?

Client: What? I don't know what you mean...

Me: <explanation of what a heat cycle is!! Seriously?>

Later...

Me: I strongly recommend that you neuter your male dog and ideally spay your female as well (discussed the possibility of pyometra, female not being the ideal age to carry a healthy litter, etc.)

Client: Oh, don't worry, she doesn't even like him!

Me: <AHHHHH!!!!!>

An "amen" sort of moment while discussing with an owner my concerns about her obese 5-year-old dog:

Me: I am very concerned about your pet's weight. She is not very old, and I am concerned about the subsequent health problems she will have due to her being so overweight. like diabetes, which is going to require insulin injections twice a day.

Client: By the power of Jesus, we are not going to have to deal with diabetes. I will talk to my mom about how much she feeds my dog.

Me: Well, I don't doubt the power of Jesus, but feeding her less is really going to help a lot.

Client: We finally went to the dermatologist earlier this summer, as you recommended, but we didn't tell you we were going.

Me: And what did the dermatologist tell you?

Client: They told us that they couldn't do any testing because we had been giving Harley antihistamines, and he needs to be off of them for 2 weeks in order not to affect any testing.

My husband was really angry that we drove all that way, and they couldn't do anything that day.

My bubble over my head: Seriously!!! I should have reiterated our conversation about having to be steroid and antihistamine-free for at least 2 weeks prior to any testing!!

Couldn't wait until after work to post this:

Me: So, during my exam of your dog, I found live adult fleas on him.

Client: Oh, I know, my wife picks them off all the time.

Me: <ANGRY FIST>

Best "question" from a group of pre-K and Kindergarten kids, after talking to them about being a veterinarian and taking care of animals:

"Yes, I was riding my bike once, and I fell, and my bike fell on me."

The client presented his dog, who had been restless and seemingly painful/uncomfortable last night. The pet was given beef round last night, and is often given beef, chicken, lamb, etc., and of course, an occasional can of Little Caesars. He is generally fed people's food only.

Me: Is feeding people/table food only your choice, or does he refuse to eat dog food?

Client: Well, it was our choice given the "Chinese food scare bullshit." He ate the beef round last night, but my wife and I ate the same thing, and we are both fine.

Me, screaming in my head: <Your dog does NOT have a human digestive system>

In the exam room with a client and her two dogs:

Client: This one has never been overweight. I don't feed the other one any more than I do this one. I think she's just big-boned.

Me: Well, then, let's take some radiographs and see how big her bones really are.

So we were sitting in Outback this evening, and I noticed the cut-out hearts on the bar for Valentine's Day. The left side of each of them was larger than the right side, and all I kept thinking was..."left-sided heart enlargement."

Just trying to maintain a sense of humor...

Repair man, entering the treatment room to inquire about how the heating system, which has been schizophrenic at best, is working: How are you guys doing in here today?

Me: Well, I have this cough and chest congestion thing I just can't shake.

Repair man: <blank look> Um, I was asking about the heat back here.

Me: <Geez, lighten up> I was joking.

Cat owner in the exam room:

Client: Can I ask a stupid question?

Me: Sure, what is the question? <Oh crap, please do not let your face betray your thoughts here>

Client: Are cats stupid?

Me: <Uh...> What makes you ask that?

Client: Well, my oven was on, and I opened the door, and the cat jumped in. My daughter said it's because cats are stupid.

Over-candid owner description of the day: an owner whose dog had an obvious mammary tumor (at least one):

Client: Look at her tit, it was hanging down to the floor earlier, and now it isn't hanging as low.

In the exam room with a little dog with feces matted around her butt...

Me: Oh my, she is quite a mess back here.

Client: Well, my husband wasn't home to clean her off before we came here.

Me: Well, we need to get you some gloves so you can clean her up when your husband isn't home.

<Oops, did I just say that out loud? My bad>

Me: What concerns do you have with <your pet>?

Client: Do you have a "pain in the ass pill" I could give him?

Me: Believe me, if I had such a pill, I would be very retired and not see your pet today!

Part Two

Oh, how I love the unfiltered client. Brought dog in for a tick on its head, turns out it's a small sebaceous cyst--nothing critical.

Me: He will be fine, it was not a tick.

Older client: This dog will not leave me alone. He's like a hemorrhoid or something--always bothering me and won't ever go away!

So vet med is not only dealing with animals, but also the owners. This woman tells me, before the son comes in, that she sometimes wants to kill her three boys LOL (I don't think literally, but perhaps?...)

Older female: I think the neighbor is teasing my dog.

Adult son: Mom, no one is teasing your dog.

Older female: You are not around all the time to see it.

Adult son: And you are always sleeping.

Interaction with an elderly woman client:

Me- So I understand that <fluffy> gets more table food than actual dog food.

Client (after a curious pause)- So, I am going to plead the 5th on this one.

Oh boy, love some client comments.

after pet

(German Shepherd) being friendly in the exam room...

Owner: I think I can take his leash off, now that I know he's not going to kill you.

Exchange between clients in the lobby--you can't make up stuff like this!

Client 1: What a cute puppy. How old is he?

Client2: 24 weeks

Client1: He is big for a 2-year-old.

Client2: He's 24 weeks.

Client1: Oh, he's 4 years old then?

Client2: No, 24 WEEKS old.

Client1: I am sorry, I am high, that's the only explanation. I would rather you think I am a drug addict than an idiot.

I had briefly forgotten about this gem from last week, from a client that is always quite animated...

Client: Do you mind if I smoke while you run the bloodwork?

Me: No, go ahead.

Client: I smoke three packs a day--smoking since I was 14. My doctor is astounded that I don't have terrible lungs. But I am probably going to die of a massive stroke or something. And it will be ugly, like I'll be on the toilet or something.

Shake your head moment. The owner presents the pet for a growth on the front paw. I am unable to see it in the exam room. I ask the owner if it's okay to take the pet to the treatment room, where I have a much brighter light, etc. The owner says, "Sure."

Me, re-entering the room: Can you please show it to me because I am unable to find it on either front paw.

Owner: Oh, it's not there now. I mean, it comes and goes, and it was there like 3 days ago. But now it is gone.

<What the what?>

Not untrue, perhaps... clever client remarks.

Me: I removed most of the hair inside his ears (the dog's ears).

Client: Oh, good, maybe he'll listen better to me now. Who am I kidding? He's a man; it won't make a difference.

Owners just keep it real in the exam room. Kind of angry kitty with GI issues...

Me: He's kind of looking at me like he's plotting my death.

Owner: More like "I am so going to shit in my carrier on the way home."

LMAO!!!

Sometimes people just feel very comfortable sharing...

Me: He (cute little puppy) seems to be already pretty bonded with you.

Female owner: Oh yes, he likes to lie right up here on my cha-chas.

Hilarious question from an owner this morning... trying to ask if the exam was over or not... The same owner also said her dog is more reliable than her nephew. LOL

Owner: So, do I keep standing here or what?

Me: You can head up front, we are finished with the exam.

Sometimes you just have to help people process things logically LOL

Me: Is "Fido" up to date on his rabies vaccine?

Client: I don't know, I didn't have him as a puppy.

Me: How long have you had him?

Client: Like 5 years

Me: Have you taken him anywhere in those 5 years for a rabies vaccine?

Client: No

Me: Ok, so he indeed then IS due for a rabies vaccine.

So thankfully I was aware of the song, but wow, what a random reference... Explaining the health and behavior benefits of spaying the pet:

Me: Also, if she is spayed and doesn't have heat cycles, you won't see random male dogs showing up in your yard.

Owner: Oh, okay, so no milkshake, no boys in the yard?

Me: Wow, uh, yes, that would be true.

Rabies observation cont'd... after both of us had to talk loudly because the dog wouldn't stop barking and lunging towards me...

Owner: Well, how much is this rabies observation thing going to cost me?

Me: Honestly, way less than if you don't do it and you then get summoned for a court appearance.

People sometimes...a woman bringing her dog for a rabies observation because it bit 3 people. Local police call to tell us they recommend a 10-day quarantine (even though the pet is up to date on rabies) rather than a Day 1 and Day 10 observation. And this is just a snip, it--the whole thing was a little bizarre.

Owner: Will someone be able to come out to the car and help me get the muzzle on my dog? He won't let me do it?

<Uh, that's a hard no--police told us one of the people the dog bit was trying to get a muzzle on the dog>

Too funny...

Owner: I spend more money on this dog than I do on my car. I am going to start riding HIS ass around town instead of driving my car!

In the exam room with a couple and their pug...

Me: Ooh, that is a flea crawling across her neck.

Wife: Oh my god, that is gross.

Husband: She's a pug; everything about her is gross.

After I give a vaccine, the client makes a comment…

Client: He didn't even move for that. He acted way different at the last vet when they put the thermometer up his keister.

I learned something new this week from a client that I never learned in vet school...

Client: "Kitten fleas" stay on the kitten and are not transferable to the adult cats in the house.

Me: Okay, that is not a thing--fleas want a blood meal, and all your other cats are at risk.

A day of client "oversharing"...

Client: Before he peed in large amounts. Now it's smaller but more frequent, just like me and my prostate issues.

A fun room from this week... older female owner with an 18-year-old cat.

Exhibit A

Me: This is a fluid-filled cyst on her shoulder. I would like to drain it with a small needle.

Owner: Last vet told me I had to wait for it to rupture.

Me: This will prevent it from rupturing.
Owner: Will it hurt her?

Me: No

Owner: It's not going to kill her, is it?

Me: Well, I certainly hope not!

Same room, Exhibit B

Owner: I buy toys for her, but she just looks

at the toys and then looks at me.

Me: What she is saying is, "Girl, I am 90years old, I don't want to play with any toys."

Oh, those clients with no filter…

Vet tech: So, what is "fluffy" here for today?

Owner: It's his f**king ears again.

K.I.S.S., right?

Owner: He has bitten my husband twice now.

Me: Was your husband doing anything in particular when he bit him?

Owner: Well, both times he was trying to rub him on his head and ears, and then on his back.

Me: I know this sounds very simple, but maybe have your husband stop doing those things to your dog.

Ah, those darn cicadas...

Client: He couldn't stop eating those cicadas. I am glad they are gone.

Me: My colleague was doing a rectal exam on a dog and thought she found a piece of plastic. Turns out it was a cicada head!

Client, to her dog: Don't shit one of those out, I don't want to see that.

The wife sends the husband with the dog for the appointment. Sorry, hubbies, but most often you are not the ones most informed about your pet's behavior/health. The wife is on the phone during the exam...

Wife: So his private area seems painful, and he is always licking there.

Me: Well, right now, he doesn't seem to mind my palpating that area to see if anything is wrong or painful.

Wife: Ha, this dog is more and more like his father every day.

Husband: <quietly just shakes his head in the corner>

Me (honestly): That is truly too much information.

Ok, let's focus... speaking to a client at the end of the appointment with his dog:

Me: What other questions do you have for me? Him: Um, do you guys need a plumber?

Me: Uh, so I take it you are a plumber?

Him: Yes, I do some freelance stuff, so if you guys need a plumber, let me know.

Me: Any questions about your dog?...

Had a client today with two orange tabby kittens:

Client: Their names are Buddy and Trump.
Me: Interesting names.

Client: They were going to be Biden and

Trump, but my wife wanted it to be Buddy, not Biden. But Trump, we kept not because we are Trump supporters, but because he's orange.

The owner presented her cat, whom she thinks is/was constipated. So many strange things in one visit...

1. Client: My cat is actually a boy cat, but I still call him SHE.

2. Client: I tried to get her to drink prune juice, but she wouldn't.

Me: Do you like to drink prune juice?

Client: Well, only when I am constipated.

3. Client: I also tried to give her a suppository--a human one, but I cut it in half.

Me: And how did that go?

Client: Not well, she didn't like it.

Oh, interesting exchange with a client today that I am pretty sure had visited the local dispensary prior to the visit, and my usual lack of filter didn't disappoint lol:

Me: So I understand she got hit by a car last week.

Client: Actually, SHE hit the car. She likes to chase them in front of the house.

Me: Well, that's why she should be on a leash when she is outside.

Client: She feels awkward on a leash.

Me: Well, she is going to feel dead when she is under a car tire.

So this reminded me of a particular client, with a pet acting a little nervous...:

Me: Has your pet ever bitten anyone?

Client: No, he hasn't bitten anyone. Well, not since the last time.

Maybe I need to be more specific when I ask a client how they are doing... Like "how are you THIS HOUR?" or something like that...

Me, entering the room: Hi there, how are you doing?

Older client: Doing okay--I have a herniated disc and haven't had surgery yet, so I can't pick up my dog. I have moved in with my son, and I don't think my dog or I like living in the basement--although it is very nice, but it's still a basement...

<Oh my>

Looking at a definite terrier/Toto looking mix, described as a chihuahua mix (NOT):

Owner: What do you think he is?

Unfiltered Me: Not a chihuahua, that's for sure. But he is really cute.

Owner: Well, you're the first person who's ever said that about him.

So yesterday, a client came in on time, but then realized she didn't have her wallet with her.

She asked if she could run home and get it. We said yes, of course. She gets back at the end of her scheduled time, and I have started the next on-time app. The tech goes in the room to get a history from the lady who has now returned WITH her wallet:

Client: I think you guys are being unprofessional, making me wait like this to be seen by the doctor.

<UGH-maybe bring your wallet next time!>

I want to post this not for empathy, but for understanding what your vet (and many other professions) go through daily. My 2nd appointment of the day died in the room with the owners, like literally passed away within minutes. The woman in the room next door had just lost a family member for whom they had been the primary caretaker. When I went back into that room next door, she apologized for leaving the room for a bit, but it was too much PTSD of sorts for her to hear the owners so audibly upset. She then asked me, "How are YOU?" I was taken aback a bit, but she said she is a therapist and can completely empathize. So just please be nice to friends, family, strangers... everyone is working through something, and kindness INDEED matters.

Awkwardly thankful...

Client (from a previous clinic): I am so glad we found you.

Me: Oh, did they tell you where I was?

Client: No, actually, my husband and I kind of stalked you on social media. He was like, "I found him and the name of the clinic."

Me: Well, I don't say this often, but thanks for stalking me.

Speaking with an elderly couple in the exam room...

Me: Do you measure his meal portions?

Wife: We sure do, but he (pointing to the husband) is the reason she is fat!

Me, to the husband: She just totally threw you under the bus and then ran you over!

Wife: And then I backed up and did it again!

Discussing (with the owner and the owner's mother) a large mass on the back of her 14-year-old dog.

Me: The good news is the pathology results show no evidence of mast cell tumor or spindle cell tumor, the malignant and invasive things I was worried about. Fortunately, the antibiotics have reduced the size of the mass, but it's still quite large.

Owner's mom: This is a damn disaster, is what this is!

Me: Yes, it kind of is, honestly.

New way to silence the corny jokesters:

I, entering the room, addressed the dog: Hi, sweetheart, how are you?

Male owner: Don't talk to my wife that way. Me: How do you know I'm not talking to YOU? Male owner: <silence>

Female owner—laughs hysterically!

Fun in the exam room. Discussing how much the owner feeds her overweight dog...

Her: He honestly gets only 1 cup of food a day with a small handful of that Fresh Pet stuff.

Me: How many treats does he get? And, just so you know, I think I already know the answer to this question.

Her: Well... probably too many.

<later>

Her: I have one more question for you, doc, and it's kind of personal, maybe.

Me: Oh, I am already married.

Her: That was not going to be my question, but you are funny!

Oh, I enjoy unfiltered clients!

#1: Client: He has these black spots on his abdomen that I think need to be removed.

Me: Actually, those are his nipples. Client: But he's a male.

Me: Well, does your husband have nipples?

Client: Oh my god, yes, and I feel like an idiot.

#2: Client: He also has those skin things on his balls? Is that what you call them?

Me: Well, that IS what they are, but some call them testicles.

#3: Client: I literally broke a sweat trying to get that cat in the carrier to get here. Did she really just walk right in for you?

Me: Yes, he really did.

Client: He's a dick, I mean, I love him, but he's a dick.

Thankfully, they laughed... me, demonstrating how to clean the dog's ears, and then I used a Q-tip to get further in:

Me: I am going to use this Q-tip now, but I don't want you to do this--not that you don't know what you are doing, but... you don't know what you are doing.

Unicorn owner, very stressed pet, didn't do well at previous vet--best affirmation of the day from a client:

Client: She has never been this comfortable at a vet. Thank you for sitting on the floor with her and letting her come to you for treats rather than getting up in her face.

Okay, here I go again... Client with a pet that has gained 10 lbs in 2 months. The pet is only 4 years old and probably 15lbs overweight.

Client: Well, at least he is young and healthy.

Me: He is young indeed, although I would argue the healthy part. Let's talk about that and why I am concerned about his weight...

A bit of humor in the exam room during a euthanasia. After sedation, the pet is oozing poop...

Owner: Can I please wipe her butt? This is undignified. And also, seriously, how are you fuc$%# breathing right now? That odor is awful!

Ugh, no filter yet again:

Client: Well, she is just a big, muscular girl.

Me: No, actually, she is fat.

Keeping it real during a behavior consultation and advocating for the puppy because... you can't just blame the pet.

Owners, with a 5-year-old child with them: So "Charlie" is the only one in the house that our puppy will nip at. He doesn't bother the other kids.

<after hearing how the child gets in the pet's face, won't leave him alone when the pet wants to be left alone, etc.>

Me: So, honestly, I am going to be very frank here. It's not just about training the puppy; it's also about training the children how to interact properly with the puppy.

Then had a nice conversation, with handouts, etc., about how to make this work for everyone.

There are daily reminders in our lives to be kind and understanding to our fellow humans. Yesterday, a woman brought her 13-year-old Retriever in because he can no longer use his back legs. The struggle for her was that this was her sister's dog, which she got when her sister abruptly passed away last Christmas Day. She felt like she was saying goodbye to her sister all over again. She needed that one person to tell her it was okay, that this was not a selfish decision, and that the decision was being made out of love for the dog and her sister. Kindness Matters!

Older woman client with her dog:

Client: Yeah, it's just me and him now. Seems like everyone else is running to the cemetery! But I am hanging in there.

Still love those clients who keep it real... her dog was given peanut butter as a distraction while I gave the vaccines. Then the dog licks her face.

Client: Peanut butter kisses are way better than... Well, ass kisses.

Client comment, describing the advice he was offered by a relative:

Client: I am here because I want your professional opinion on what is going on with my dog. I got some advice from a relative, but let me just say, well... she doesn't remember the last thing she doesn't know everything about.

So, best compliment/affirmation of the week, from a new client, with a Great Pyrenees …

Owner: You are literally on the floor with my dog. I saw your picture on the website with your Pyrenees, and I knew this would be a great fit. You totally "get" my dog.

I had one of those days where pet owners were very unfiltered, and I felt like I was back in my bartending days lol. One hilarious experience from today:

Me: We can follow up by phone initially and see how "fluffy" is doing.

Female Owner: Oh, good, that will save me some money. Or otherwise, I am going to be at Club 380 (local strip club, apparently) on that pole! And when people ask my name, I am going to say "Dog Lady". (as she is swirling her hand above her head)

This is so very well said...

"Pets, it turns out, also have last wishes before they die, but only known by veterinarians who put old and sick animals to sleep.

Twitter user Jesse Dietrich asked a vet what the most difficult part of his job was.

The specialist answered without hesitation that it was the hardest for him to see how old or sick animals look for their owners with the eyes of their owners before going to sleep.

The fact is that 90% of owners don't want to be in a room with a dying animal.

People leave so that they don't see their pet leave. But they don't realize that it's in these

155

last moments of life that their pet needs them most.

Veterinarians ask the owners to be close to the animals until the very end.

"It's inevitable that they die before you. Don't forget that you were the center of their life.

Maybe they were just a part of you. But they are also your family. No matter how hard it is, don't leave them."

Don't let them die in a room with a stranger in a place they don't like.

It is very painful for veterinarians to see how pets cannot find their owners during the last minutes of their lives.

They don't understand why the owner left them. After all, they needed their owner's consolation.

Veterinarians do everything possible to ensure that animals are not scared, but they are completely strangers to them. Don't be a coward because it's too painful for you.

Think about the pet. Endure this pain for the sake of their sake.

Be with them until the end.

One of those moments when you know you need to go to the next exam room, but the person in the euthanasia room just needs to talk and process things. A 20-year-old cat--so not tragic, but sad nonetheless--but the owner is talking about how they had this particular cat BEFORE they even had children. Precious moments in an otherwise sad moment--just nice to be able to "be there" for that person who really needed it.

Entering room with a 100lb German Shepherd here for vaccines-previously marked as "muzzle--does well with owner" (note from 3 years ago):

Me: Hi, how is K.C. doing today?

Owner: Good, and don't worry, he's only bitten one person before.

Me: Okay, but it wasn't his previous vet, was it?

I love it when clients keep it real...

Me: This is a yeast infection in the ear. Client: Oh, it's not ear mites?

Me: No, the debris you see from ear mites

looks like dry coffee grounds. This is more like...

Client: Gross brown gooey crap?

Me: Perfect description!

This was not one of those "out of the mouth of babes" things; it was a grandma talking about her dog's obsession with cleaning himself and why she didn't ever neuter him:

Grandma: I got him when he was 2 years old, and I didn't want to put him through that surgery, so now he walks around with everything just hanging out. And he is also all the time licking that little sucker, too!

Sometimes... The owner brings his dog for an exam and vaccines. He found the dog in the street after he had left work one evening.

Client: He is 8 months old.

Me: Based on his teeth, I think he is likely more like 10 months to a year old.

Client: Well, I had him at a vet 2 months ago, and they said he was about 8 months old.

Is it wrong that I am secretly amused when the tech comes out of the room after getting the history on an appointment and basically says, "Just so you know, these people are pretty much bat shit crazy?" LOL

New clinic, new material...

Me: So she (cat) is pretty clingy to you?

Owner: Yes, this one is always up my ass, and that one is always up my daughter's ass. I can't go anywhere in the house without her following me.

Awkward (and hopefully subtle enough) correction in the exam room, with a pet with a likely urinary tract infection:

Client: I was told by my previous vet that her uvula has extra skin, and that's why she might get recurrent infections.

Me: <ok, don't laugh, don't laugh, just use the correct word, no need to correct HER specifically> Well, yes, she does have a hooded VULVA, which indeed can predispose her to urinary tract infections.

Tough week of lab results and a reminder to be nice to people in your daily encounters-- and my week is NOT uncommon for my many colleagues... having to tell the owners of a 10 month old dog that their dog's mass is a subcutaneous hemangiosarcoma (poor prognosis), a mast cell tumor in a dog whose owners are dealing with cancer in their other dog, and a 4 year old Great Dane with not only a likely nasal carcinoma but also tested positive for heartworms, and then going into rooms and being excited for owners who have new adorable new puppies. So just a reminder to be nice to everyone--you never know what they are going through.

I often see the meme of "be nice, you never know what someone is going through," and it resonated with me today. While talking to an owner about his being conflicted about euthanizing his 15-year-old dog.

Me: I don't think that it is the wrong decision or a selfish one for you to help <Fluffy> move on to a place where he is not scared and not suffering.

Owner: Thank you for saying that. Since we lost our mom, I have been trying to maintain a household and raise my little brother. It has all just been a lot.

I love clients with no filters... 15-year-old cat presenting for quality of life concerns and likely euthanasia. The cat has been urinating all over the house, loss of appetite, etc., all likely related to failing kidneys-- honestly, it was time...

Me: So he is still urinating everywhere?

Client: Yes, and not eating. And honestly, doc, he's also just an asshole. He's my asshole, and I love him, but he's an asshole.

Some descriptions I get in the exam room are... interesting:

Client: I think her hips and knees are fine because she can do her exercises with no problem.

Me: Exercises?

Client: Yeah, well, she humps her bed a lot.

That's not how it works... Client presenting with a 20.8lb cat that weighed 9lbs in 2021, and is now not even 3 years old:

Unfiltered me: Wow, he has gained a lot of unhealthy weight in a year and a half.

Client: I know, it kind of happened overnight, like 6 months ago, we thought he was getting a little chunky, and now he weighs 20lbs.

So usually, I am the one in the exam room without the filter... I was explaining to a client where exactly in the ear to place the ear medication bottle tip so that it goes into the vertical canal:

Me: So it's going to go in this sort of outermost hole you can see.

Owner: Wow, there are so many "that's what she said" things in that statement.